T0144013

AuthorHouse™
1663 Liberty Drive
Bloomington, IN 47403
www.authorhouse.com
Phone: 833-262-8899

Because of the dynamic nature of the Internet, any web addresses or links contained in this book may have changed since publication and may no longer be valid. The views expressed in this work are solely those of the author and do not necessarily reflect the views of the publisher, and the publisher hereby disclaims any responsibility for them.

This book is printed on acid-free paper.

ISBN: 978-1-6655-3968-5 (sc)
ISBN: 978-1-6655-3967-8 (e)

Library of Congress Control Number: 2021919958

Print information available on the last page.

Published by AuthorHouse 09/29/2021

authorHOUSE®

To my son, I know this has been a crazy experience, but I want you to know that I am always here for you. If ever there is a tomorrow where we are not together, there is something you must always remember. You are braver than you realize, you are stronger than you seem and smarter than you think. But the most important thing you need to remember, is that you are not alone in this fight, and that I love you forever and always!

A mother was waiting for her little boy to come out of heart surgery.

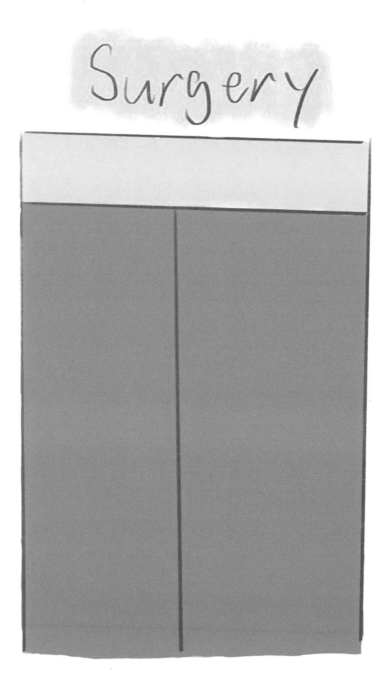

Suddenly the elevator doors opened and she heard, "Would the parents of Orion please come up?"

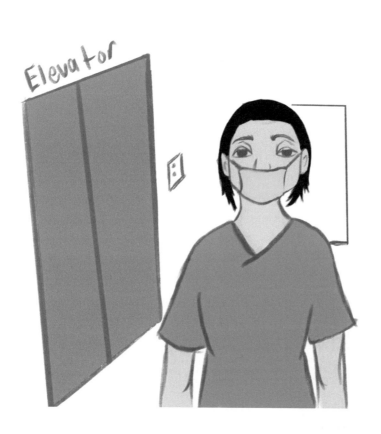

The nursing staff ushered the mother to his room. "He was waking up, said the doctors."

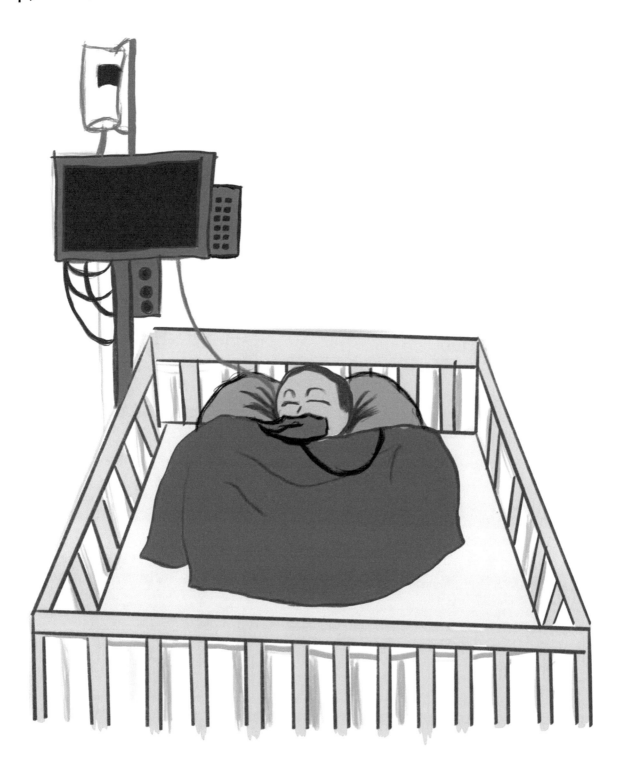

As he opened his eyes, he thought "Where is my momma?" He scanned the room, but she could not be found.

He could not move. He could not cry. "So, I will have to look around the room with my eyes to find my momma," he thought.

As his eyes began to focus, he could not tell who his mother was, as they were all wearing masks.

He saw a woman. "Is she my mom," he thought.

The nurse was checking his vitals but did not say a thing.

The nurse was not his mom.

Then he saw another woman, "Is she my momma?" he thought.

"This little guy did really good in surgery," she said. "Now I do not expect to see him for another five to ten years."

The nurse was not his mom.

The surgeon was not his momma. So the baby looked on.

"I want my mom!" he thought. "But where? But where could she be?"

Then his eyes came to another person. "Are you my mom?" he thought.

"I will be taking care of you today, little man," he said.

That person's voice sounded to deep. "That is not my mom," he thought.

The nurse was not his mom.

The surgeon was not his momma.

That person was not his mom.

So, the baby boy continued to look. He saw another person.

"Are you my mother," he thought.

"He seems good. We can go ahead and remove the breathing tube," he said to the group of people.

The nurse was not his mom. The surgeon was not his momma, and neither was those two other people.

"Was momma even here?"

"I need to find momma! Everything is so scary. Why can't I move? He thought. "Who are these people? What are they doing to me? I WANT MY MOMMA!"

At this time, his breathing tube was taken out, so he was able to cry for his momma. But still did not see her.

Then he spotted a computer on wheels. Could that be his mother? No, it could not. But then he spotted someone looking over it.

"There she is!" he thought. He cried, but the person did not move. The person continued to type.

A computer was put in front of his face with a woman on the other end. She looked and sounded familiar, but she could not be my momma. "Momma is here, somewhere I know it," he thought. He hoped.

The screen went black and then another person came on. But the boy knew that was not his mother. If dad was there, then mom must be here.

Dad continued to speak, but he was not looking at me. "Who was he looking at," he thought.

Then brother came on and kissed the screen.

And another person. These facetimes were long. They went on and on. "All I want is my momma," he thought.

Get me out of here!

Just then, he heard his mom's voice. He began to cry, "Momma where are you," he thought. "I want you to hold me!" Then something happened. A warm hand took his.

"I am here. You are okay, my baby boy."

"Oh, momma, it's you," thought the baby boy. "You are not a nurse, you are not a surgeon, you are not a computer or in the computer." "You are my momma," he thought with excitement and he squeezed her hand in return.

I love you my little warrior!

Real Heroes wear masks. To all the Doctors, Nurses, Paramedics, and all health workers that selflessly fight to protect our community, thank you!

The General Concerns

Accept any help that is offered to you and your family: Parking Passes, Extra Food, Gas Cards, Sleeping Arrangements, etc. An exhausted, stressed parent will have difficulty being supportive for a hospitalized child.

When you have questions or concerns about your child, don't be afraid to ask. Write down your questions, and even the answers if it helps. Ask about medications, in-home treatments, future, what-ifs, etc. You want to be as familiar as possible.

Your discharge instructions should include signs and symptoms to watch for that may indicate a change in your child's condition. Normally, your doctor will schedule the appropriate physicians follow-up appointments before you leave the hospital (whether it be close to the hospital or close to your residency).

Make sure you have contact numbers to call during the day, at night and on the weekends if questions or concerns arise. If something doesn't seem right, question it, as you are your child's voice when they are young.

Siblings of hospitalized children often have difficulties of their own that need to be recognized. They often feel left out or forgotten because of the large amount of attention on their sick sibling. They often can be just as scared, worried, and or jealous of the attention their brother or sister is receiving. Spending time with other family members does help, but depending on the age of the child, this will soon be inadequate substitute. (If for some reason you cannot be present, at least try to phone, video chat or facetime the other child to make them feel recognized.)

These suggestions are only general recommendations. You should evaluate your own situation and decide what is best for you and your children. If you are unsure what to do, discuss your concerns with the hospital doctors, social workers, and or nurses caring for your children. They will help you make an informed decision.

My Notes
on Congenital Heart Defects

Congenital Heart Defect is a malformation of the heart

CONGENITAL ANOMALY IS AN ABNORMALITY PRESENT AT BIRTH.

Echo is a picture of the heart and vessels.

Murmur is a noise made by blood flow, which may or may not be abnormal.

Cyanosis is the blueness of the skin when their isn't enough oxygen in the blood.

Echocardio is a diagnostic method in which pulses of high frequency sound, called ultrasound, are transmitted into the body and the echoes returning from the heart and other structures are made into an electronic picture.

Diastolic Blood Pressure is the blood pressure inside the arteries when the heart muscle is relaxed.

Open Heart Surgery is surgery performed inside the heart with the aid of a heart-lung machine.

Dysrythmia (Arrhythmia) is an abnormal rhythm of the heart.

CHD has no cure and requires life long medical care.

CHD is the world's #1 Birth Defect. Affecting 1 in 100 babies.

85% of CHDs have no known cause and 15% are genetic (runs in the family).

Normally the aorta comes from the left lower chamber of the heart, the left ventricle. The aorta is the largest blood vessel in the heart and carries pink blood from the heart to all parts of the body. When the aorta is described as overriding, it means that the vessel is inappropriately positioned and straddles both the right and left ventricle just above the ventricular septal defect. ★

85-90% of children born with CHD are Living into adulthood

When the pulmonary artery, the artery that carries blue blood from the right ventricle to the lungs, is blicked, the condition is called pulmonary stenosis.

★

VSD is a hole between the two lower pumping chambers of the heart.

Pulse Oximeter is a noninvasice sensor that is clipped to a patien's finger or toe to monitor blood oxygen levels.

A CT SCAN IS A COMPUTERIZED X-RAY PROVIDING CROSS SECTIONAL PICTURES OF THE CHEST.

★

Tetraology of Fallot aka. Blue Baby Disease is a combination of four different heart problems: Pulmonary Stenosis (PS), ventricular septal defect (VSD), overriding of the aorta, and right ventricular hypertrophy.

Your child may not meet milestones.

The term 'tetralogy' comes from the Greek word for 'four'.

Ventilator is a mechanical device that ventilates the patient by providing air to and from the lungs.

Heart Warriors

The right ventricle is the lower chamber of the heart that pumps blue blood to the pulmonary arteries. Normally, the RV muscle is thin. Hypertrophy means the muscle wall of the chamber has become thickened. This occurs in TOF, because of the extra work the muscle must do to pump blood past the blocked pulmonary artery as well as pump blood to the high-pressure aorta.

Hypertension is commonly called high blood pressure, meaning above normal range.

Tricupsid Valve is the heart valve between the right atrium and right ventricle, comprised of three flasps or cusps.

Carditis is the inflammation of the heart.

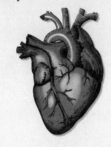

Cardiologist is a specialist in the diagnosis and treatment of heart disease.

ATRIUM IS ONE OF THE TWO UPPER CHAMBERS OF THE HEART.

Anoxia means literally no oxygen.

CATHETER IS A THIN FLEXIBLE TUBE THAT CAN BE GUIDED INTO BODY ORGANS.

Heart Lung Machine is a special instrument used to provide circulation to the body during open-heart surgery.

Atrium Septum is the muscular wall that divides the left and right upper chambers of the heart, called the atria.

Cardiac pertains to the heart. Sometimes refers to a person who has heart disease.

A Blue Baby has a blue color tint to their skin, called cyanosis, caused by insufficient oxygen in the arterial blood.

Cardiology is the study of the heart.

Bradycardia is an abnormally slow heart rate Generally, anything below 60 beats per minute.

You are more than your diagnosis.

CHD or not, we are all human beings. We have loves, losses, activities, work, education and our human connections. And while this disease can be absorbing, terrifying or debilitating to your participation in the world; keep being strong!

Cardiovascular is pronounced Kar-dee-oh-Vas-kyoo-lur ★

Your child should be okay to play normal sports.

A CARDIOLOGIST WITH SPECIAL TRAINING IN ELECTROPHYSIOLOGY (HEART RYTHM ISSUES) IS CALLED EP CARDIOLOGIST.

A fellow is a physician who has completed their residency and is completing additional training in a specialty area.

Heart disease isn't contagious – you cannot catch it like you can COVID, the flu, or a common cold.

Remember Nurses are the hospitality of the hospital.

Long Term Risks may include delay of milestones, growth delays, ADHD, and learning disabilities

An attending physician is a member of the hospital staff who has completed their residency.

APN (Advanced Practice Nurse) or NP (Nurse Practicioner is a registered nurse with an advanced master degree who has specialized in the care of cardiac patients.

CHD patients are brave with every heart beat.

A physician who specializes in cardiac care is called a Cardiologist.

 There are Facebook Groups out there that can help support you and your family.

The best person to tell how your child is feeling is your child.

Cardiac Surgeon specializes in the care of pediatric congenital heart disease.

Tetraology of Fallot is pronounced Te-tral-uh-jee of Fal-oh

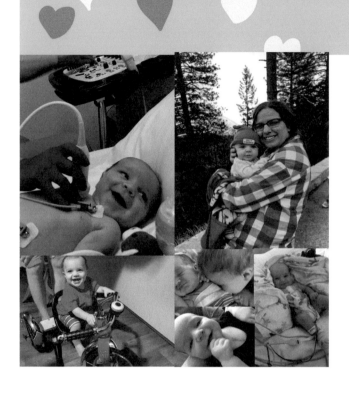

Childhood Heart Facts

Living with CHD

Most people with CHD do NOT look sick, but they fight every second of the day, just to live! Beneath their shirts are battlescars, which are a constant reminder of their courageous fight. Only mended, never cured!

1 *About 1 in 4 babies born with defet has a critical CHD (also known as congenital heart defect).*

2 *Babies with a critical CHD, need surgery or other procedures in their first year of life.*

3 *If children do not have symptoms, they often develop in the first few weeks after birth. Common symptoms include:*
- blue color around lips, nails, & blue skin (called Cyanosis)
- fatigue
- pale skin
- shortness of breath
- poor growth
- tiredness when feeding

Additional Resources

The Children's Heart Foundation
www.childrensheartfoundation.org

CHD_Hearts
beacons.page/chd_hearts

Organized Chaos Life
www.organizedchaoslife.com

UCSF Benoiff Children's Hospital SF

American Heart Association
www.heart.org

Conquering CHD
conqueringchd.org

Vanderbilt Pediatric Heart Institute

AuthorHouse
www.authorhouse.com

Please note that Internet URL's may change without notice

Printed in the United States
by Baker & Taylor Publisher Services